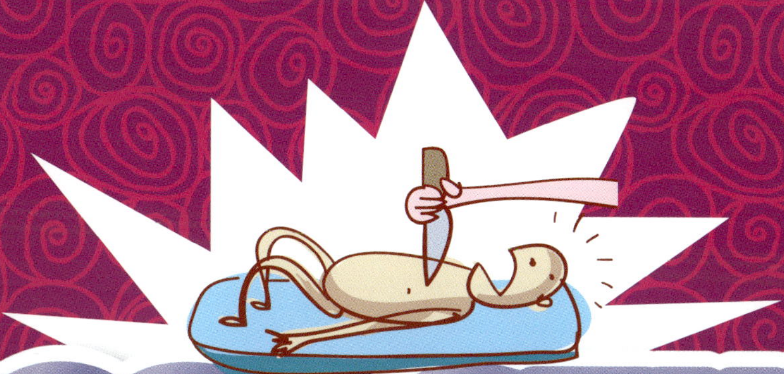

GROSS STUFF IN THE HOSPITAL

BY PAM ROSENBERG

ILLUSTRATED BY BEATRIZ HELENA RAMOS

ABOUT THE AUTHOR:

Pam Rosenberg lives in Illinois with a husband, two kids, two cats, a hermit crab, a few bugs, and lots of bacteria and other tiny things she doesn't like to think about.

ABOUT THE ILLUSTRATOR:

Beatriz Helena Ramos is an artist from Venezuela who lives and plays in NYC. She works from her animation studio, Dancing Diablo, where she directs animated spots. Beatriz has illustrated a dozen books and she particularly loves gross stories.

The Child's World

Published by The Child's World®
1980 Lookout Drive • Mankato, MN 56003-1705
800-599-READ • www.childsworld.com

Photos: Dmitry Kalinovsky/Shutterstock.com: cover; MedstockPhotos/Shutterstock.com: 19; Shamleen/Shutterstock.com: 17; Tatiana Shepeleva/Shutterstock.com: 10

ISBN 9781503850224 (Reinforced Library Binding)
ISBN 9781503850675 (Portable Document Format)
ISBN 9781503851436 (Online Multi-user eBook)
LCCN: 2021930073

Printed in the United States of America

TABLE OF CONTENTS

UGH!

SOME PEOPLE ARE GROSSED OUT BY THE SIGHT OF BLOOD AND A TRIP TO THE DOCTOR'S OFFICE FOR A CHECKUP.

Others love going to the emergency room and like to watch when the needle goes into their arm for a shot! Read on to find out if you're cut out for a career in medicine or a lifetime as a squeamish patient.

HOSPITAL DRACULAS

Did you know that there are people at hospitals that do nothing but go around **taking blood from people?** Yes, these medical Draculas are called **phlebotomists**. They spend their days sticking very sharp needles into people's veins and collecting their blood in little tubes. The blood is then sent to labs to be tested. There are lots of different kinds of blood tests that can give doctors important clues about a person's health.

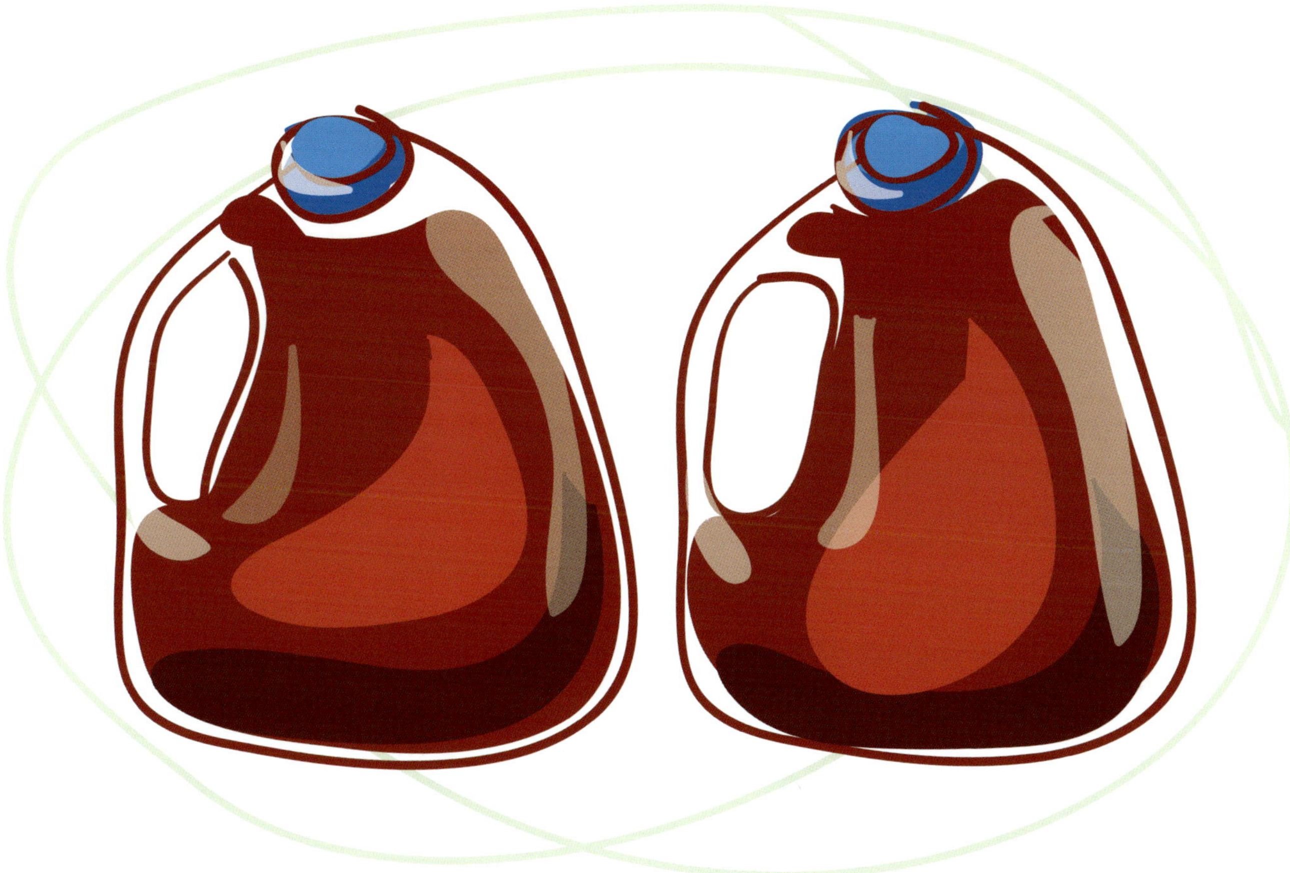

Did you know that **blood makes up about 10 percent of your body weight?** An adult has somewhere between 10 and 15 pints (about 5 to 7 liters) of the slimy red stuff flowing through his or her body. Newborn babies only have about a cup (about .2 liters) of blood.

SCALPELS AND STITCHES

Surgeons are doctors that cut people open. Sometimes they repair body parts. Other times they take out diseased body parts. The earliest surgeons cut people open without knowing much about what would happen if they did. There were no drugs that knocked people out. **A patient would lie on a table fully awake** while a surgeon used a sharp knife to cut him open. Even scarier, **back then, doctors didn't know about germs.** They didn't wash their hands before doing surgery and they didn't wear rubber gloves. Sometimes they even went from one patient to the next without washing their hands. You've probably guessed that there weren't too many people who survived those early operations!

Today surgeons know a lot more about the human body. But they **still cut people open with very sharp knives,** called **scalpels**. Sometimes they also use things like saws to cut through people's bones. And if you need brain surgery, first your head is shaved and your scalp is cleaned. Then the surgeon cuts through your scalp to get at the bone underneath. Then a special drill is used to make a hole in your skull. A piece of bone is removed so the surgeon can get to your brain. After surgery, the bone is usually put back in place and your scalp is stitched closed.

Did you know that brain surgery is one of the oldest kinds of surgery? Archaeologists have found evidence that brain surgery was done thousands of years ago in Europe, South America, Africa, and Asia.

Many people who go to the hospital emergency room need stitches. Doctors call them **sutures** and they are **used to hold skin and other organs together after they have been injured or after surgery.** The first stitches were made from the intestines—or guts—of sheep. This kind of suture was good because it would break down and be absorbed by the body after a few weeks. Today most absorbable sutures are made from man-made materials and not animal guts. For some stitching jobs, doctors need sutures that won't be absorbed by the body. Those sutures are made from **silk** or artificial fibers such as nylon and polyester.

GERMY STUFF

There are lots of sick people in hospitals. And lots of sick people can mean lots of germs, otherwise known as **bacteria**. These tiny living things are so small, you need a microscope to see them. Lots of them live on and in our bodies and don't cause problems. But some of them are real bad guys. One **bad bacteria** that can make people sick in hospitals is called *Staphylococcus aureus*. These little round germs **can cause some major problems such as infections** of the lungs, heart, and brain. They **can also cause some minor but yucky problems** such as pimples and boils. A boil is a **pus**-filled lump on the skin that looks kind of like a giant pimple. Sometimes the pus—a yellowish-white liquid—oozes out of them. A patient with a serious case of boils will need to take antibiotics—drugs that will kill the bacteria that caused the boils.

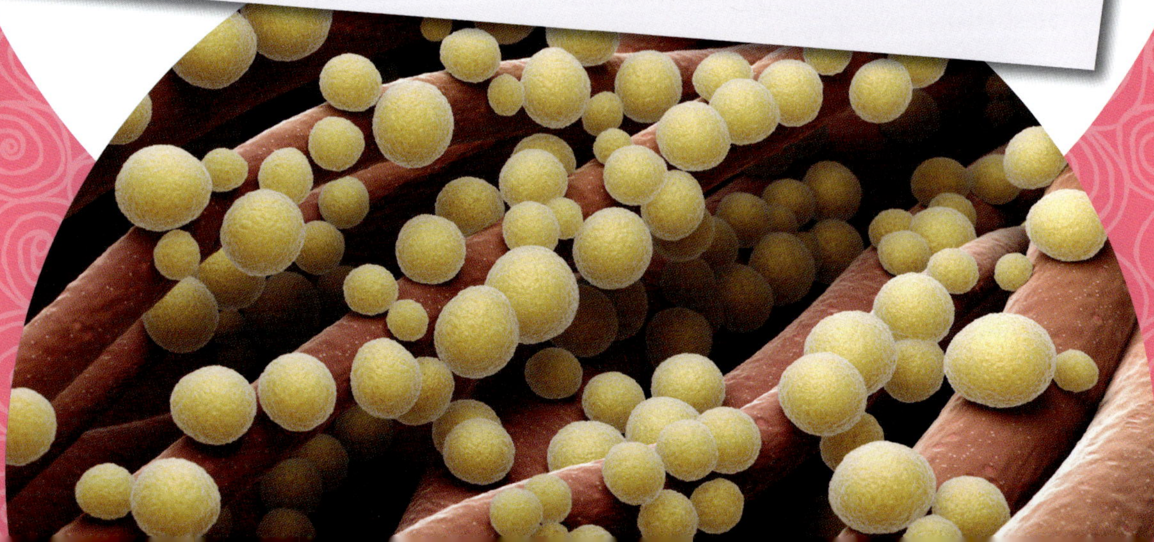

Speaking of pus, **want to know what that yucky goo is made of?** There are special white blood cells in your body that fight bacteria. When you get an infection, these cells flood the area and devour the bad bacteria. Then they die. The gooey pus is made up of the **dead white blood cells and dead bacteria.**

Some kinds of *Streptococcus*, another type of bacteria, can also send people to the hospital. One kind of Streptococcus causes **strep throat.** You may have had this disease. Its symptoms include a REALLY sore throat and a fever. But strep throat is nothing compared to another infection that can be caused by a form of Streptococcus bacteria known as **Group A Streptococcus.** That nasty infection is called necrotizing fasciitis (NEK-ruh-ty-zing fash-ee-EYE-tiss) or **flesh-eating disease.** But the bacteria don't really eat flesh. They release poisons that destroy skin and muscle **tissue**. Doctors prescribe strong medicines for patients with necrotizing fasciitis. They also have to cut away lots of dead tissue to help stop the infection. In really bad cases, a patient may have an arm or leg cut off to stop the spread of the infection. But don't worry, this kind of infection is rare.

People who work in hospitals spend a lot of time keeping things clean and trying to get rid of germs. This is important because some kinds of bacteria are very **hardy**. In one study, one kind of *Staphylococcus* **bacteria survived for up to 90 days** on some commonly used hospital materials such as the fabric used for the drapes you can pull around a patient's bed!

BODY PARTS

People who work at hospitals sometimes have to handle body parts. For example, sometimes organs such as kidneys or livers become diseased. Then they may not work the way they are supposed to. When the patient gets really sick, he or she might need a transplant to stay alive. **A transplant is when a healthy organ is cut out of one body and sewn into another body.** Some organs for transplants can be taken from living donors. These are people who agree to give up one of their kidneys or part of their liver. Other organs, such as hearts, are taken from the bodies of people who have died.

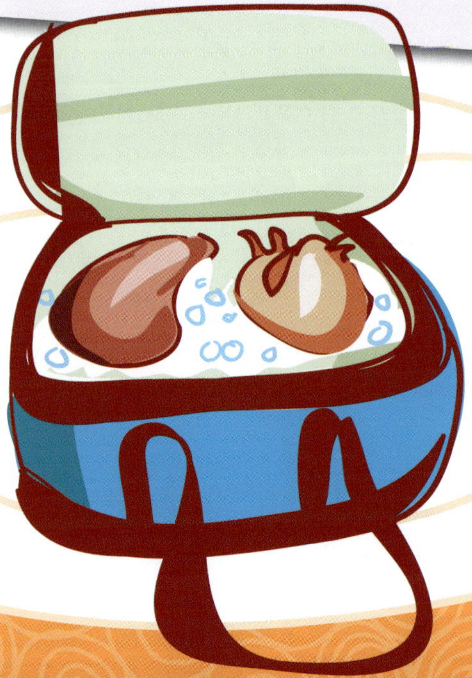

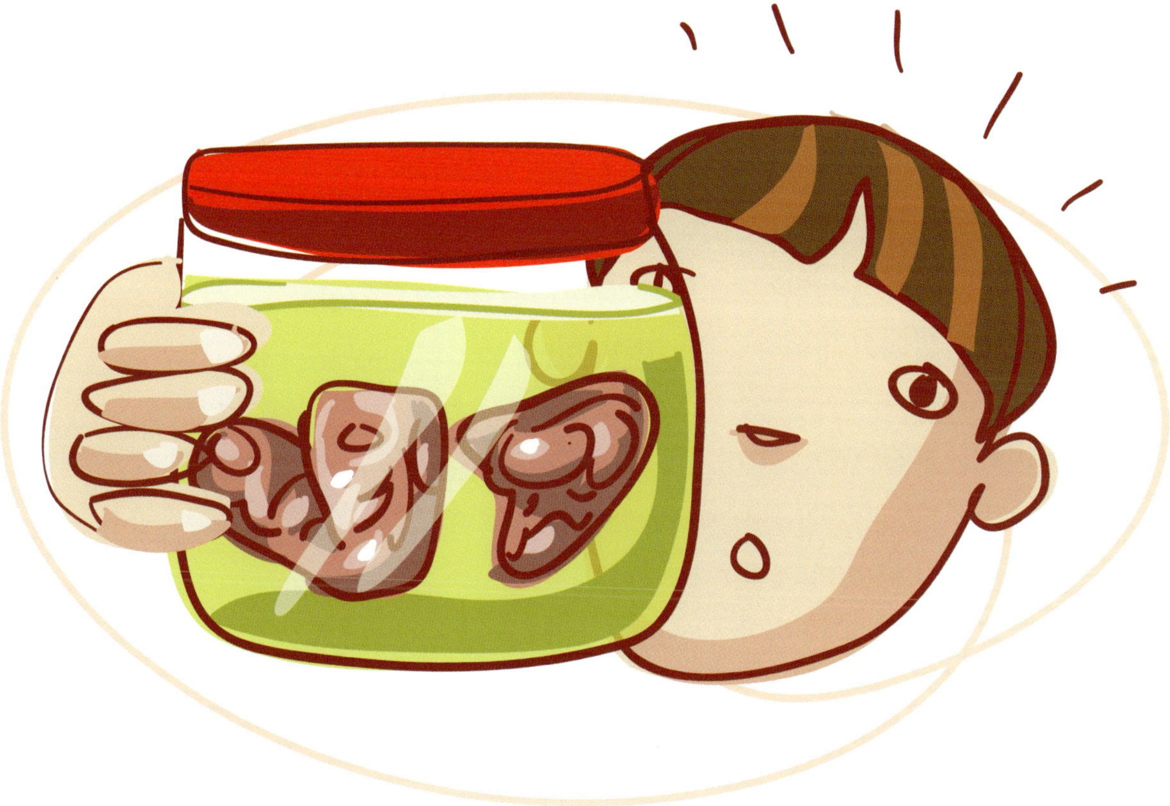

What happens to diseased body parts that are removed? They can't just be tossed in the nearest trash can and taken out to a dumpster. Most of the time, the removed body parts are sent to special medical waste management sites where they are burned. **Some people ask if they can keep their body parts.** Depending on the hospital's rules, they may be allowed to bring their tonsils or other organs home with them. Imagine going over to a friend's house and seeing tonsils in a jar in the living room!

What happens if somebody loses a body part that he or she didn't mean to lose? Maybe your dad puts his hand too close to the blades of the lawnmower, or your mom's hand slips while she's chopping up meat for dinner. Somebody is missing a finger. The best thing to do is to seal the finger in a **plastic bag and place it on ice.** Then get to the emergency room, pronto! Depending on the injury, it may be possible for surgeons to sew the finger back on. First the surgeon reconnects the **arteries** to get the blood flowing into the finger again. Next, the **veins** will be reconnected so blood can flow out of the finger. If the veins aren't reconnected, the finger will swell up with blood and that can cause more damage to the finger. Once the blood vessels are sewn back together, the surgeon starts reconnecting the **tendons**, bones, and nerves.

Once the surgery to reattach a finger (or other detached body part) is complete, **doctors sometimes bring in some creepy crawlers to help their patients recover.** What are these medical creepy crawlers? Bloodsucking **leeches**! Yep, sometimes after the delicate surgery to reattach a finger is completed, blood can accumulate at the spot where the finger was sewn back on. This isn't good because it can cause damage to the finger and surrounding tissues. This is where the leeches come in. **Leeches love blood.** So doctors place leeches on the finger and the little bloodsuckers dig in and start sucking the patient's blood. They gorge themselves on blood until they are about ten times the size they were when they were placed on the finger. Then they fall off. All of this probably sounds disgusting to you. But I bet that if it could help you save your finger, you might be begging your doctor to put some leeches on you!

GOING POTTY

Did you know that the average person **pees about two pints** (almost 1 liter) of **urine** each day? And just because you are in the hospital doesn't mean that you stop peeing. So what do you do if you can't get out of bed to use a toilet? You have to use a **bedpan.** It's a plastic or metal container, kind of like a big dish you put under your bottom. Then you pee in the container while you are lying in bed. When you are done, someone has to come and take the container full of pee away and dispose of it.

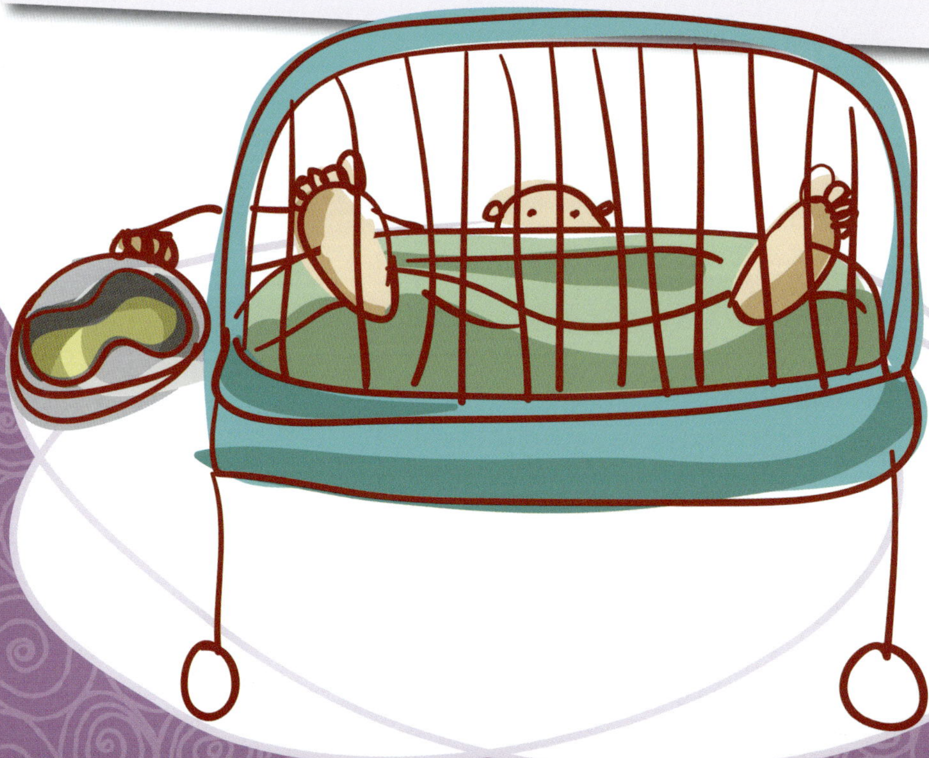

Sometimes patients have to use a special tube to get rid of their urine. The tube is called a **catheter**. A catheter is inserted right into a patient's bladder. The pee flows down the tube, out of the body, and into a bag that is attached to the patient's leg or resting next to the bed. When the bag is full, it is emptied. This method makes using a bedpan sound like fun, doesn't it?

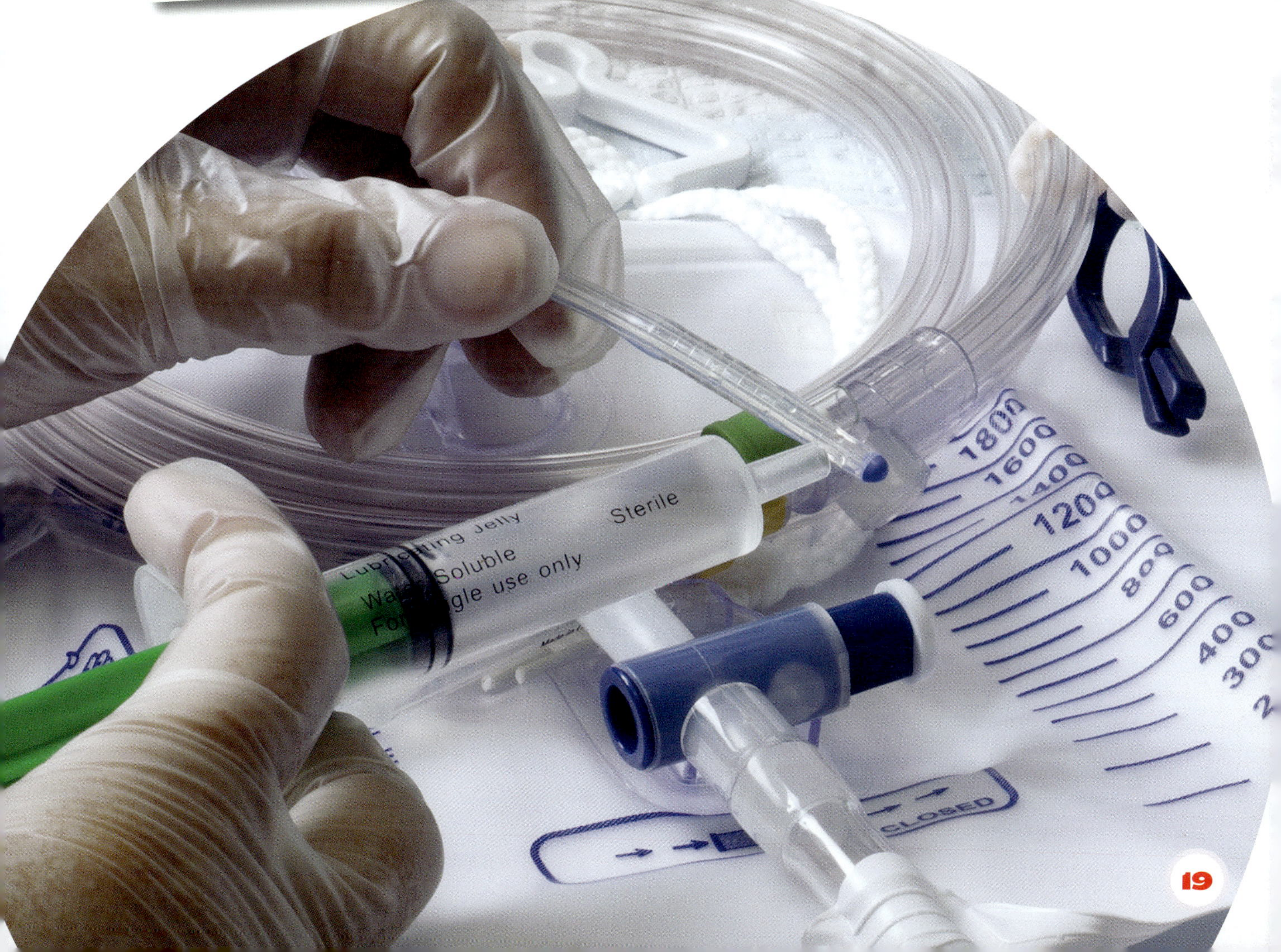

So does a career in medicine sound like a dream come true to you? Or are you thinking that you never, ever, EVER want to go near a hospital? **Blood and guts aren't for everyone,** but if gross stuff fascinates you, a hospital may be just the place for you!

GLOSSARY

archaeologists (ar-kee-OL-uh-jists) Archaeologists are people who learn about the past by digging up old buildings and objects and studying them. Archaeologists have found evidence that brain surgery was done thousands of years ago.

arteries (AR-tuhr-eez) Arteries are small tubes that carry blood from your heart to all the parts of your body. Doctors can perform surgery to sew arteries back together if they are cut in two.

bacteria (bak-TEER-ee-uh) Bacteria are microscopic living things. Some bacteria cause diseases.

catheter (KATH-uh-ter) A catheter is a tube that is inserted into the bladder to drain urine. Some hospital patients must use a catheter instead of a bedpan or a toilet.

hardy (HAR-dee) If a living thing is hardy, it can survive for a long time under difficult conditions. Some hardy bacteria can live on surfaces for as long as 90 days.

leeches (LEECH-ez) Leeches are worms that feed by sucking blood from other animals. Doctors sometimes use leeches to drain blood from body parts after surgery.

phlebotomists (fleh-BOT-uh-mist) A phlebotomist is a medical professional who draws blood from patients for testing.

pus (PUHS) Pus is a yellowish liquid that comes out of wounds or sores on the skin. Boils are large bumps on the skin that are filled with pus.

scalp (SKALP) The scalp is the skin covering a person's head. Doctors cut through a patient's scalp when they do brain surgery.

scalpels (SKAL-puhl) Scalpels are small, very sharp knives used by surgeons. Surgeons use scalpels to cut into a patient's body.

silk (SILK) Silk is a fiber that is produced by silkworms. Some sutures are made of silk.

sutures (SOO-churz) Sutures are fibers or threads used to close wounds in the body. Some sutures are made of nylon or polyester.

tendons (TEN-duhns) Tendons are strong bands of tissue that attach muscles to bones. Surgeons sometimes have to reattach tendons and muscles after a severe injury to a hand or other body part.

tissue (TISH-oo) Tissue is a group of similar cells that form a particular part or organ of the body. Some bad germs can destroy muscle tissue.

urine (YUR-in) Urine is the liquid waste that you pass from your body. Bedpans are special containers made for collecting urine.

veins (VAYNS) Veins are small tubes that carry blood back to the heart from other parts of the body. If a finger is cut off, doctors can sometimes sew the veins and arteries back together.

FOR MORE INFORMATION

Bennett, Howard. *The Fantastic Body: What Makes You Tick & How You Get Sick*. Emmaus, PA: Rodale Kids, 2017.

Bradley, Timothy J. *Strange but True: Gross Anatomy.* Huntington Beach, CA: Teacher Created Materials, 2013.

Mould, Steve. *The Bacteria Book: The Big World of Really Tiny Microbes.* New York, NY: DK Publishing, 2018.

Olson, Gillia M. *Muscles and Bones: A Repulsive Augmented Reality Experience.* Minneapolis, MN: Lerner Publications, 2021.

Visit our website to learn more about gross stuff in the hospital:
childsworld.com/links

Note to Parents, Teachers, and Librarians: We routinely verify our weblinks to make sure they are safe, active sites—so encourage your readers to check them out!

INDEX